LEADERSHIP DEVELOPMENT

Copyright ©2021 by TVC Publications LLC.

All rights reserved, including the right of reproduction in whole or in part in any form. No part of this book may be reproduced in any form without written permission of the publisher.

The Values Conversation ©2021 and TM
TVC Publications LLC.

ISBN 978-1-956737-00-4

Cover design copyright ©2021 by TVC Publications LLC.
Cover design and interior art by Tracy Dorsey

Book design by Patrick Dorsey
Typeset in High Tower Text and Conduit ITC

TVC Publications LLC
9051 Watson Road, Suite 165
St. Louis, MO 63126

Manufactured in the United States of America

LEADERSHIP DEVELOPMENT

JEFF ARTHUR

WITH PATRICK DORSEY

TVC Publications

This book is dedicated to Todd Spittal.

A great friend and one of the greatest leaders I have had the privilege to work with.

Thank you for the opportunity to learn from you over the years.

Contents

Introduction 1
Take Care of Yourself First 3
Make People Better Through Your Leadership 5
Be Approachable 7
Define Your Terms 9
Trustworthiness: Key in Leadership 11
Great Leaders Are Great Students 13
Leaders Must Have Emotional Intelligence 15
What's Your Plan of Action? 17
Have a Sense of Humor 19
Find a Mentor 21
Use Your Peer Support 23
Pass Along What You've Learned 25
Pull the Trigger! 27
Delegation in Leadership 29
Do the Big, High-Impact Jobs 31
Things Don't Always Work Out 33
Leadership and Continuing Education 35
Building Relationships 37
Create Solution Finders 39
Fresh Eyes 41
Do Your People Trust You? 43
Your Job's to Inspire 45
Setting the Example 47
Setting the Vision 49
Keepin' It Real 51
Help Them Make a Difference 53

Help Your People Make a Difference 55
Looking for Leadership 57
Looking for Connection 59
People Want Stability 61
Pareto Principle People 63
Proper Employee Training 65
Leadership and Juggling 67
Shutting Up 69
Taking a Breath 71
Gather the Information First 73
Make Sure Your People Are Heard 75
Appreciate Your People 77
Never Embarrass Your People 79
Focus on Building Strength 81
Push Yourself 83
What's Your Opinion? 85
Influence 87
Developing Leaders Around You, Part 1:
Characteristics Leaders Must Have 89
Developing Leaders Around You, Part 2:
The Quality of Gratitude 91
You Get What You Expect 93
Being a Leader and Friend 95
Leadership Focus: Your Strengths 97
Dealing with People 99
A Lesson on Purpose from *The West Wing* 101
Who Have You Influenced Today? 103
Training 105
Define Communication 107
Focus on Strengths 109

- Give Feedback 111
- Multiplicity of Leadership 113
- Learn from the Leaders Around You 115
- What Are You Prepared to Do? 117
- Pull the Trigger 119
- Get the Job Done 121
- Being a Leader 123
- Understand Your Leadership Strengths 125
- Communication Details 127
- Strengths and Weaknesses 129
- Abundance of Resources 131
- A Leader's Role 133
- Take Responsibility 135
- Fostering the Right Kind of the Team 137
- Don't Have All the Answers 139
- Proper Timing 141
- Provide Direction 143
- Learning Never Stops 145
- Stuck Behind an Inferior Leader 147
- Problem People 149
- Bottlenecks 151
- Are You a Manager or a Leader? 153
- Making the Key Decision at the Key Time 155
- Solving Problems 157
- Lead Through a Turnaround 159
- More Success, More Problems 161
- The Weakest Link on Your Team 163
- Emotions and Decisions 165
- Make Do With What You Have 167
- Step Up 169

Watch Your Mouth 171
Self-Awareness 173
Getting Along with Your Team 175
Know the Winds 177
Walk Them Through It 179
About the Author 181

Introduction

While creating *The Values Conversation: Leadership Development*, I had two types of leaders in mind:

- The *up-and-comers*, the leaders who are learning and developing and looking for bite size morsels of leadership information and insight to learn from
- The *seasoned veterans*, the leaders who are confident about leadership from their years of experience but are looking for quick reminders of things they've learned throughout their years as leaders

Because there are literally thousands of great leadership tools out there, from so many great leaders, it's easy to become overwhelmed figuring out just where to go or specifically what to look at. This book is designed to be easy to read, easy to reference, and easy to apply in the various different leadership situations you, as a leader, face every day.

I've always envisioned a reader of this book sitting somewhere, sipping their morning coffee while reading the day's consideration, reflecting on the reminder and contemplating how to apply it to their own team.

Whether you read it all at once in one sitting or treat is as a "daily thought" and focus on only a page a day, I hope that this book helps in solidifying your leadership foundation—the rock upon which everything else you do will be built upon.

Take Care of Yourself First

One of things I see over and over and over again with executive leaders is *multiple responsibilities*. This is a constant concern and constant problem for them. They're switching hats all the time from publicist to marketer, putting out fires with their employees, working the books at night, ordering whatever is needed.

If you're running your own business, you've been there (you may still be there). And you know keeping up with all the different responsibilities you have feels almost impossible—Burnout and exhaustion are the two things every leader and small business owner deals with and faces.

We all know that the first thing we should do in this situation (and is lost on so many small business owners in this position) is to take care of ourselves. But it's so hard for us to do that. Instead, we tell ourselves we're the owner, we're the executive, we're *the leader*—and nothing in our business is going to happen if we're not there doing our job.

But you can't do your job burnt out and exhausted.

So whenever you find yourself out of balance and overloaded—emotionally, physically, mentally, or spiritually—make sure you get yourself to a place where you're at your best, so you can do what you need to do for everyone else.

It's a bit like the oxygen mask instructions flight attendants always give when you're on an airplane waiting to take off: "Please place the mask over your own mouth and nose before assisting others."

To help others, take care of yourself first.

Make People Better Through Your Leadership

What is leadership?

There are great definitions from Maxwell, great definitions from Ziglar, but the most basic concept to understand about a leader is that we, as leaders are helping other people become *more*.

Leaders help their people develop, help them grow, helping them understand or work through a project or whatever the challenge is. In fact, if we as a leader you're *not* helping other people become more, you're not an effective leader.

One of the greatest statements on leadership I ever heard is, "If you think you're leading people and you turn around and no one's following you, you're not leading anyone. You're just going for a walk."

That's not where you want to be as a leader.

Recognize that no matter what you're doing with your business, no matter what you're doing with getting stuff out the door for your customers, no matter what you're doing to accomplish any other duties, your leadership should be giving them an example to follow to become greater in some way.

This is your first responsibility as a leader: to help the people around you become more, to become better, and to become something that they never thought possible.

Be Approachable

I have some shocking news for you.

Are you ready?

You're really not as important as you think you are.

That's kind of scary, I know. But what can happen with leaders is we begin to think we've arrived—and all of a sudden we're thinking that we're all that and a bag of chips, and nobody around is really worthy compared to those of us in charge.

The truth of the matter is that's not the way it works.

True leaders—great, effective leaders—are approachable. Their people can come to them, talk to them, ask questions, make mistakes, and ask for support.

While as a leaders you must be firm and set the direction and lead the way, you also have the responsibility to love and support and show understanding to those you lead.

If you come across as above it all and unapproachable, as someone who can't be bothered with *that,* you're not leading.

You're doing harm.

You're harming our company and our industry. You're harming your people whom you say you want to make a difference for.

And ultimately, you're harming yourself.

Be the leader your people can come to.

Define Your Terms

One thing I find frequently with the different executives and leaders I coach and consult with is communication problems.

Not all the same problems, mind you—communications problems play out in a thousand different ways. But a great example is one you see on almost any TV sitcom from the last 50 years

You know the formula: whether it's *I Love Lucy* or *Friends* or *The Office,* two characters begin talking and it's clear to the audience they're talking about two different things, but neither character realizes it.

Hijinks and hilarity ensue.

Except when it happens in a real-life company—particularly your company. Then, there's no hijinks and no hilarity when a miscommunication.

There's only lost time and lost money. Depending on how much, there's also finger-pointing, anger, and resulting distrust. Attitudes get broken and people get upset.

"I thought you were saying..." says one person.

"But I thought you meant..." says the other.

As a leader, you can't put enough focus on making sure that when communications are flying back and forth that everyone is talking about the same thing, with terms all defined up front so everyone understands what they mean in the same way.

You need to be sure your people do this.

Set the example.

Trustworthiness: Key in Leadership

Think back to a time when you were working with or working for someone whom you loved working with. Now think back to a time when you were working with or working for someone whom you just couldn't stand.

I'd be willing to bet you that the person you got along with so well and anyone else you enjoyed working with throughout your career, were all people you trusted. You trusted their decisions. You trusted their input. You trusted their *intentions.*

The one you recalled you didn't like working with? Probably not so much.

Trustworthiness is so important and is so incredible in the business world. And somehow it's glossed over—if not downright ignored—in most business coaching. As I work with executives, one of the key things we talk about is trustworthiness. In his book *The Five Dysfunctions of a Team*, Patrick Lencioni asserts that the number one dysfunction that teams struggle with is absence of trust. Why is this important? Because, as Lencioni discusses, without trust teams are incapable of full discussion and debate and hesitant to express conflicting opinions, which results only in poor decisions and inferior outcomes.

Our organization, our people, need an environment of trust as a foundation for successful teamwork. We, as leaders, must live a life—personal and business life—that sets the example of trustworthiness.

Be the person your people can trust.

Great Leaders Are Great Students

I read an article once that pointed out how people who are successful are willing to suspend everything that they think they know about a subject and are willing to learn.

That goes right in line with the most basic teaching of leadership: *Great leaders are great students.*

Great leaders want to learn. And great leaders continue to learn. They read. They go to seminars. They attend motivational sessions and do whatever they can find to hear something new and to get a different perspective to learn and grow and become *more* through exposure and involvement with both mentors and peers.

One of the most important things to understand as a leader is that we never know it all. We never become so important or so expert that we can't step away from what we think we know to allow someone else to teach us.

When you grow more as a leader, the more our people around you can grow and the greater your organization's potential becomes.

Keep growing.

Leaders Must Have Emotional Intelligence

I want to encourage you as a leader to think about something that maybe you haven't thought about a lot, a term you're hearing used more and more today: *emotional intelligence.*

It is so important for a leader to have emotional intelligence.

If you're unfamiliar with the term, a basic definition is: *the ability to be aware how and understand that emotions, both our own and others', drive and impact our behavior and the behavior of those we interact with.*

As a leader, this ability is simply critical to your success. For example, when your people come into the workplace, it would be nice if they could leave everything from home "at the door" when they arrive, wouldn't it? But realistically, they don't do that. They can't. The argument they had with their teenage child is still with them... The problem they're struggling with in their marriage is right there... Their aging parent's health issues are weighing on them...

As a CEO, a manager, or a small business owner, you *must* have emotional intelligence not just to recognize what's going on with your team members, but to be able to help them, support them, and still get the best out of them as they face their struggles.

Just as important, as a leader you have to have emotional intelligence about yourself. You have to know what it is that triggers you, what's going on in your own life that you're dealing with, and what struggles of your own are affecting you. It's hard to recognize and admit these things about ourselves, especially when you're a leader and you feel your team is relying on you to be stable and ready to take on anything.

But nothing will demoralize a team more than a leader who is out of touch with his or her own emotions—and doesn't realize how it affects the team.

Know who you are and how you affect your team.

What's Your Plan of Action?

One of the things that I work on when coaching and training executive leadership is helping them create a personal plan of action for their own personal life.

As John Maxwell says in his book *How Successful People Grow,* "Growth rarely happens on its own." Growth, he says, has to be intentional and has to be developed on purpose. There has to be a desire to go out and learn and to put a plan of action in place just for growth alone.

Whenever we as leaders are growing—physically, mentally, spiritually, and emotionally—our people, grow as well. But that growth can't happen without a personal plan.

Decide that you want to grow.

Have a Sense of Humor

Want to connect with your people? Have a sense of humor.

I'm not talking about a sharp, cutting wit. I'm not talking about sarcasm. And I'm definitely not talking about coming across as a jerk while you're trying to be funny.

Neither am I suggesting you become the next Robin Williams.

Rather, I want to challenge you to work on developing a sense of humor about what you're doing, about what you're about, and most importantly, about yourself.

Self-deprecation goes a long way.

Whenever your people see that you can laugh at yourself—particularly at the mistakes you make—you're letting them know that it's not always serious and it's not always life-or-death

Show them that sometimes we can just enjoy ourselves on the journey.

Find a Mentor

If you don't have one already, please, please, *please* find yourself a mentor.

There are so many things that we as leaders and business owners understand. There are also so many things that we as leaders and business owners do not understand.

One of the things that we can do for our own sake—and for the sake of our company—is to find somebody who's been there and done that and is willing to work with us to help us develop and become *more*.

More what? More capable, more understanding, more efficient, more self-aware—whatever it is we're lacking and they can show us how to improve.

Find somebody you trust. Find somebody who's been through the war that have been in the trenches that have been fighting the fight that you're fighting and has learned some tricks to fighting it and get that person to agree to mentor you. Not only will having this guidance and insight reduce the number of mistakes you make, it will diminish the scale of the ones you do make. And at the same time, whenever you're struggling with something or your abilities just hit the wall, you'll have this person to talk with to help find a solution to what it is you're struggling with.

I, in fact, have multiple mentors for different areas of my life, different people who I can go to for answers and help depending on what aspect of my life I need help with.

Seek out people you can turn to when you need them.

Use Your Peer Support

Be sure to engage with the people who are your peers in the industry. Business owner, leader, CEO, whatever your role, it's important to have your peer support group around you.

When we're in the trenches and either get hyperfocused on the stuff in front of us or realize we've started making mistakes, we start to seclude ourselves. Almost instinctively, without even realizing it, we begin to pull away.

That's where your peer group can help. People who've been where you are, they know what you're dealing with. They can support you, help pull you out of the isolation you've created for yourself to re-engage, and understand what's happening how you can more effectively handle it.

Reach out to your peers, and learn from them.

Pass Along What You've Learned

This may sound a little crazy. Once I make this suggestion, I know there's a good chance you'll say to yourself, "Oh, no—there's no way I have time for that!"

Hear me out...

The benefits of what I'm asking of you are innumerable, and the positive impact on your professional life will resonate throughout your career.

Find somebody in your industry, somebody you like and connect with, and teach them the things you know.

Become a mentor.

"Oh, no—there's no way I have time for that!"

It's not just for the person you'll be mentoring. It's for you. Again, hear me out...

I first heard this thirty years ago and I've seen it proven true a thousand times: teaching forces us to know our stuff better.

It really does make sense: when I have demonstrate or explain something, I have to know the subject inside and out—not just the *what*, but the *how* and the *why*. And sharing those insights? That's where it really becomes interesting—and fun.

Find somebody you know, who you connect with and who wants to learn and grow, and take the time to teach them what you know.

You'll both benefit.

Pull the Trigger!

We want to do the right thing all the time. Especially in our role as a leader.

But because of this desire, end up afraid to "pull the trigger" as we wait for everything to align properly and fall into place before we take action.

While there's a lot to be said for making sure of the information you need, your understanding of the cost, your grasp of what changes are going to result, there's also a point where you caught up in "analysis paralysis" and end up stuck where you are and unable to move forward.

So let me tell you this: If you need to make a change, *make a change.*

Don't worry about everything being perfect—nothing is *ever* going to be perfect, and if you wait for it to be perfect... well, let's just say you'll be waiting a long time.

And not moving forward that whole time.

So what if you made a mistake the last time? That was last time. This time's different—different circumstances, and a different you who's grown and changed since that last time.

Count the costs, understand what needs to be done and what changes will result. Then go ahead and do it.

Pull the trigger!

Delegation in Leadership

We often get confused about delegation.

The truth of the matter is, leaders often become concerned about delegation because they're afraid.

Afraid of appearing they aren't doing enough. Afraid of whatever is going on not turning out exactly right.

Afraid of losing control.

The truth of the matter is that, as John Maxwell explains so well, the more delegation you give, the more you trust your associate. The more we trust the people working with you, the more they respect you and see you as the person who can lead them

The more you give away, the more you receive back.

And it's very important as a leader to understand that it's okay to delegate out to your people.

That doesn't make it less frightening. You have to know your people, and sometimes you only learn about them through trial and error. So some of those times you delegate…sometimes they're not going to quite work out.

But that's much better than trying to hold on to—trying to hoard—all the responsibility and do everything yourself. You have to delegate and let them take some of the responsibility.

It's the only way for all of you to grow in skill experience and most importantly, in trust with one another.

Let your people do their jobs.

Do the Big, High-Impact Jobs

There are jobs that only you—the leader—can do, and only you, the leader, should do.

These jobs you want to keep to yourself are the big impact projects that you don't ever want to delegate. The ones you don't ever want to ask other people to do.

The jobs your people look to you to do because you're the leader.

This is why you delegate other jobs that others can do. You don't want to expend and exhaust yourself on the things your people can handle. You need hold yourself in reserve for those jobs that only you, out of everyone in your organization can take on. Make sure you have the time, energy, and focus to tackle those big, high-impact jobs.

The ones the leader is supposed to take on.

Things Don't Always Work Out

Things don't always work out.

At least not the way we think.

If you're like me, oftentimes when you hit a milestone or road sign, and you step back and start thinking. You reflect on how you got where you are, how things have worked out, and how this part of the plan happened but this other part didn't...

I was talking to one of my clients whose company had grown 400% over the last couple of years. As he and I were talking, he said something that I thought was incredibly profound:

"You know, I guess we got here... But is this where I wanted to be?"

You see, where he was—where he found himself—was in no way where he'd expected to end up. He was the leader. He'd groan his business and he'd set the goals and the direction. But when he looked around, he wasn't seeing what he'd expected.

As leaders, we set the goals. We set the direction. And we think it's going to work out a particular way.

And so many times it doesn't.

You can establish objectives and you can plot and implement the ways to achieve them.

But keep in mind: on the journey, things may not work out. Which is why you want to make sure you have values underneath you to stand upon and help you know at any time who you are and where you're going.

Leadership and Continuing Education

I don't know about you, but a lot of times I get caught up in being "about the business"—worrying over what's the next thing, putting out the next fire, heading off the next crisis, making sure we hit this objective, overseeing payroll...whatever.

We forget that, as the leader, we need to be about more than the business. To keep our knowledge and abilities where they need to be for us to lead, we have to keep learning.

When was the last time you worked to learn something new? Whether something about your industry or leadership or team building, or communication?

Often, we think we know it all—or at least enough. But the reality is that, after being the leader for a while and having so many people turn to us so often, we forget that we don't know so much. Whether emotional intelligence or dealing with team dysfunction, it's important for us to continue to grow and learn and become stronger and more knowledgeable across the board, not just in certain aspects of our business.

Set goals. Make the time. Find ways to educate and grow yourself so you can better lead your people.

Building Relationships

My fiancée, and went on a trip to Napa Valley and we loved it. We visited all sorts of wineries, large and small. There were ones that were in caves and stored all their stuff underground, and there were some private wineries that you can't get even into unless you know somebody (or somebody who knows somebody) who can get you invited to visit. But the assortment of wineries, the sheer number of them...it was just incredible.

We were discussing it later, all the places we liked, the ones we didn't like, the stuff we all had going on. And as we talked, I realized something fascinating: The wines didn't matter.

What mattered to us and stood out in our memories of each winery we visited wasn't the wines was the relationship that was built between us and the winery's host. Whenever they connected with us, we had a great time and we bought a ton of wine. But when a host was pretentious or conceited or just plain acted like a jerk while we were visiting, we couldn't wait to get away quick enough, no matter how much we loved the wine there.

The lesson: build relationships with your people. That's what counts and matters most.

Create Solution Finders

General Colin Powell once said:

"Great leaders are almost always great simplifiers, who can cut through argument, debate and doubt, to offer a solution everybody can understand."

He's exactly right.

So many times as leaders, we get called into stuff we've neither prepared nor planned on being called in for. Not just the fires and the crises and the whatever else, but those things that can only be solved by seeing the big picture, understanding our people have the emotional intelligence to recognize what's really going on, and then cutting through all the details and distractions to find a simple solution that everyone understands and agrees with.

Now, that *is* a tall order. Maybe you can't get everybody on board. Maybe there have been too many problems. Or too many hurt feelings. Or too many whatever.

But the responsibility of a leader is to *lead*. Particularly, to lead our people from crisis mode and problem mode to solution mode. Especially today, when so many people want to be victims, a leader must understand how to get everyone involved in a situation past focusing on the issue and get them focused on the solution.

Lead them to where they can become solution finders.

Fresh Eyes

Have you ever been around two-year-old?

I suspect you probably have, and you're familiar with the incredible "*Why? Why? Why? Why? Why? Why? Why? Why? Why? Why?*" that just makes you want to plug your ears or put the child in another room or send the kid to Grandma's or *something*.

Think about it, though. Two-year-olds ask those incessant questions because they don't know *why*. They've only been on earth for two years, know virtually nothing, and are seeing many things for the first time, with fresh eyes.

Leaders need to have that same perspective looking at their businesses. Like a two-year-old, they need to look at everything with fresh eyes and ask questions:

Is this the right process?

Why is this here?

Where do we add value?

Why are we seeing resistance to this in our organization?

Is this the right direction?

Does this need to be adjusted?

Is there a way to do this faster or less expensively?

Should we discuss this?

Why are we doing it this way?

Is there a better solution?

Step back, and look at your business like a two-year-old. With fresh eyes.

Do Your People Trust You?

A certified parent coach I know told me once that when parents he's coaching explain to him that they can't trust the decisions their child makes, it isn't about whether the parent can trust the child or not.

It's about the child figuring out whether they can trust the parent or not.

That seems backwards, doesn't it?

But the reasoning behind it make sense: A child who hasn't determined if he or she can trust a parent can't trust that parent's reactions, judgment, or advice when making a decision. The kid wonders, Will my parents overreact? When my parents tell me they're going to do something, do they? When I do something wrong, are they consistent in how they react?

The same thing is true in your business.

Do your people trust you? Do they trust your judgment? Do they trust your reactions to the daily goings-on?

Or when they bring you a problem or a failure?

If you don't think you can trust your people's decisions, take a look and see if they can trust you.

Your Job's to Inspire

Former NBA coach Phil Jackson once said:

"You can't force your will on people. If you want them to act differently, you need to inspire them to change themselves."

What a tremendous truth.

Especially for a leader, because at the end of the day, our job as leaders is to inspire our people to become better because they want to be better.

You have to lead them to choose to be better. And the scary part of that is, the only way you can do it is by setting an example yourself. You have to show then what's out there, and show them that it's possible to achieve and improve.

You can't force them. Well, you can, but that will only be a short-term gain. Requiring everyone in a certain role to acquire a PMP will result in all those people getting that certification. But it will end up just being part of the job, something they're expected to do. You won't change their behavior. And you certainly won't change their thoughts.

You need to inspire them to accomplish that.

Rather than trying to force them, be the person they want to be like. Inspire them to grow through your own learning and your own growth.

So ask yourself this: Am *I setting the example for who I want my people to become?*

Setting the Example

Every business book and every business coaching program, whether about leadership or team-building or communication or whatever big idea or buzzword is being covered, stresses the essential importance of leaders setting the example for their people.

Yet somehow, as leaders, we seem to struggle constantly with this.

And for no good reason. Every time you're walking around the place you work or engaged with one of your teams and things aren't going quite right, you have an opportunity to model for those folks exactly how you want them to handle things when they're in a similar situation.

Set the example—What are you doing? What are you saying? When you're in a situation on front of your people, do what you'd want them to do.

And if right now you're saying to yourself, "But I'm the boss. What I do isn't what I want my people doing." Guess what? You *are* showing them what to do. If you handle things one way and expect your people to handle them another, there's always going to be disconnect between you and your people. And you're always going to see struggles

Look at your own example.

Setting the Vision

Do you know what the vision of your company is?

I'm not talking about a mission statement. I'm not talking about a wall of multiple paragraphs. I'm talking about something that can be printed on a t-shirt.

This is the vision.

It's the single most important thing to start with—it's the purpose for your company, and reason you brought these people together to what you're all doing. The vision is so critically important because it states simply what you're doing, how you're doing it, and you're applying to achieve your goals.

And when you and your people all understand these things, everything becomes so much easier and simpler because every decision at that point comes down to only two questions: *Which way will help us accomplish our vision?* and *Which way will help us stand on our values even more?*

Can you rally your people to the vision of your company?

Keepin' It Real

As a leader, if you're a phony, you're dead.

One of the key words more and more used in business today is *authenticity*. While it can get overused, the truth of the matter is *authenticity* carries extraordinary power.

Are you being authentic with your people? Are you open with them? I'm not talking about sharing things you shouldn't share (and if you don't know what the line is between what you should and shouldn't share, you probably shouldn't be the leader).

But recognizing your vulnerability with your people —just a little bit—goes a long way.

They don't have to know all the things you struggle with, but it helps when they know that you have your own struggles, too. If one of your people is really challenged by working out a project schedule and you honestly tell that person "You know what? I had a rough time the first few times I attempted a schedule like this. Want to know how I got it figured out?"

Help them know that you're human, too.

Help Them Make a Difference

Every one of our associates that work with us wants an opportunity to make a difference.

Everybody wants the opportunity to stand out—not just personally, but so they can see the work they do helps the company stand out and become more successful.

We see it over and over and over again from sports teams to political organizations, to rallies, to volunteer groups and whatever else.

People want to be part of something bigger than themselves.

Whenever your people have the opportunity to advance and to make a difference in the company, they're going to try that much harder. If there's no hope of ever making a difference, of helping something or somebody, they'll be hard pressed to ever try.

People look for opportunities to make a bigger difference. They're hungry for it.

Help them find the ways to make that difference.

Help Your People Make a Difference

Every one of our associates wants the opportunity to make a difference.

They want to stand out not only for making a difference at what they do in their jobs, but for what the company they work for does. Whether it's sports teams, political parties college affiliations, people want to be involved with something bigger than themselves.

As workplace leaders, we recognize that need to stand out whenever we promote our people when they've made a difference. More than advancing that person's career, promotion not only acknowledges that a person has made a difference, but provide that person the opportunity to make an even bigger difference.

What's your vision for your company? How are your people supporting and advancing it?

How can you provide them the opportunity to make a difference and advance it?

Looking for Leadership

Have you ever seen the movie *The American President*?

There's a point in the story where Michael Douglas, as the President of the United States, is verbally sparring with his aide, played by Michael J. Fox. They're going back and forth and Fox says something incredible about people and leaders:

> *"They want leadership. They're so thirsty for it they'll crawl through the desert toward a mirage, and when they discover there's no water, they'll drink the sand."*

If you're a leader in your organization, if you're in any position of authority, right or wrong your people are looking to you to lead them.

When the unexpected happens, they're looking to you to take charge, set the direction, and be the example of how they need to proceed through whatever the issue is. And as the movie says, they'll all crawl through the desert for that leadership—true, authentic, caring leadership that makes them want to be a part of what you're doing.

Without that leadership, there's no way your organization is ever going to reach its maximum potential.

Do you supply real leadership for your people?

Looking for Connection

Often we just take for granted—or we assume we understand—what's going on in the lives of the people we work with.

The truth of the matter is, we usually don't.

But the people who work for us, they're looking for connection. Do you, as leader, understand what their job is? What it entails to be done right?

Do you understand the challenges they face just to get to work every day? How many buses are they catching? How much car trouble they have? How many kids they have to have to drop off at how many schools before heading to work?

Do you make sure they understand that you care about their life outside of the business? Or do they believe you see them just as a number on a resource sheet or just a warm body or they just somebody to fill the spot in the organization.

Until you—the leader—connect with your people, and until your people realize that you actually do care, you're never going to get the most out of them. Whether that means productivity or focus or getting the most out of their talents, it won't matter because as far as they're concerned, what's the point if you don't care about them?

Why should they care about you?

People Want Stability

According to recent surveys, the number one thing people are looking for in an employer is stability.

People want to know that their job matters and that is going to be here for them. They also want to feel that they're a part of something bigger and that the organization's leadership values them and is connected with them.

They want to know that the work environment is one they can rely on and safely pour all their effort into it—nobody's going to give their all to a job that won't be there down the road.

But that's not the only stability they crave. They also need stability from you. As the leader, you can't afford to be kind Dr. Jekyll one moment and beastly Mr. Hyde the next. If your people don't know who their leader is, they're going to worry too much about which one—Jekyll or Hyde—they're going to get in any given interaction, and they're not going to be able give you their all.

Provide your people stability so they can give you their 100%.

Pareto Principle People

Named for Italian sociologist and economist Vilfredo de Pareto who defined the rule, the Pareto Principle states simply that 80% of results are produced by 20% of causes. This can include situations and results such as:

- 20% of employees are responsible for 80% of their company's results
- 20% of a manufacturer's shop hazards cause 80% of its shop accidents
- 20% of a company's products make up 80% of its sales

When you understand this rule, you also come to realize that, in general, 20% of your people are doing 80% of the work.

Let that sink in. Do you know who they are?

As a leader, then, you need to determine who the people you and your business rely on are. Write a list of who you consider to be all your key people, and then ask yourself the question *If any of these people were to leave, which one's absence would damage our organization?*

The names you come up with are the people you're depending on—the 20% doing 80% of the work. Th. And they're the ones you need to connect with, make sure they feel your organization is stable, and set example for them as the leader because you're getting your greatest return from them in your business.

Pour your energy into those people.

Proper Employee Training

In all different organizations I've worked with over the years, the problem I've seen over and over is the disconnect between what the employees do and what their training says they're supposed to do.

You wouldn't think it would be that different, would you? But once you start digging in a little bit, you realize that either the people either weren't trained, or they were trained and promptly told once they were in position, "That's the training—this is how we really do it to get the job done."

Meanwhile, the leader is drifting through the building, happily thinking blissful leader thoughts about strategy and goals, completely unaware that his people don't know how they're supposed to be doing their jobs or what's expected of them.

If your people aren't trained properly or aren't doing their jobs according to the approved training, they have no foundation for their job to build on. So not only are they doing their job incorrectly, but they have no way to make a difference in their job, no way stand out and possibly advance because they're not doing it right.

Help your people be successful in their jobs. Train them correctly.

Leadership and Juggling

As leaders, we have to juggle a lot of different things. The important part is understanding which of those things are key and how you keep your focus on them while juggling.

A great friend of mine was a performer, and once he and I were talking about jugglers. "Do you know how you get good at juggling?" asked me once. I shrugged.

"Practice."

When you're the leader, you have to juggle. There are some projects we can delegate. There are some projects that we can delegate but need to keep an eye on. And there are some projects we need to do ourselves. We have to juggle those things.

All the time.

And the only way to learn to do it? Practice.

Which means you'll be learning. Practicing to get better. And making mistakes. Sometimes, you'll keep all the tennis balls in the air. Sometimes, you'll drop the bowling ball, sometimes, you'll drop the chainsaw.

On your foot.

More than a couple times.

Yes, you're going to look stupid. But you'll be learning, becoming a better juggler, becoming a better leader by developing your ability to keep an eye on all the tennis balls and apples and bowling balls and chainsaws you have in the air.

All the opportunities, all the projects, and all the decisions.

Are you juggling correctly?

If not, start practicing.

Shutting Up

You're not as smart as you think you are.

It may be difficult for you to hear, and I'm sorry to be the one to tell you.

But it's important to understand that you don't have all the answers. None of us do. I don't have all the answers—ask my team, they'll tell you that I'm not as smart as I think I am.

You're not either.

If you stand on your own and you become an Island off to yourself, you're going to limit yourself with what you can do. As a leader, it's important to know not just when to ask for help, but *how*.

It's important to connect with the people who you need to connect with. It's important to understand that—whether it's another business owner, or another leader in what you do, or a business coach or personal coach—somebody somewhere can mentor you, can support and teach and help you.

Other people are very skilled and very smart in what they do. Use their education. Use their knowledge. Use their wisdom.

Learn from them.

Taking a Breath

If you don't stop occasionally and replenish or recharge, you're in trouble.

Stopping to take a breath this way runs counter to the way we do as leaders—keep on pushing and pushing and driving our organization forward.

I don't know of a leader that I've ever met. That doesn't struggle with this somehow because we don't, we don't know when to quit. And we were trying to do the next thing. We're trying to get the next [00:00:30] project done. We're trying to put out the next fire. We're trying to help the next person. We're trying to, whatever it is (you fill in the blank), but we don't take time for ourselves. Or for our children and family—the people closest and dearest to us.

Because we're out trying to take care of everything else, all at once.

Go through that list of, all those things that you think are so important, the ones you think aren't; going to get done—or done right—unless you do them. None of these things will happen unless you take care of yourself.

Stop, take a breath, relax, and take care of yourself.

Today.

Gather the Information First

Making sure you gather all the information before you make a decision.

I can't tell you how many times I've screwed that up. I'm very much a "fire-ready-aim" kind of guy. If I can get it done quickly and get out of the way and get on with my life, that's how I'm going to do it.

But whenever I do that, every time I make a decision too quickly, it always comes back to bite me on the backside.

As a leader, you probably have the same tendencies I do—grab the bull by the horns, take the plunge, just run with it—to just do what you have to in order to get whatever it is done right now.

And I bet it comes back to bite you on the backside.

When a new decision confronts you, It's often a good idea to get ask a question, read up on it, or get another viewpoint to make sure that what you're thinking is the right way to go.

Take a breath and decide to gather more information.

Make Sure Your People Are Heard

As leaders, we forget sometimes how important it is to our people to be heard.

In the business world especially, people want to be heard because it's an indication of respect—"You respect me enough to hear my view, to listen to my thoughts on this. You don't necessarily have to act on it, but if you just hear what I have to say, then at least I know that I have value to you and our organization."

If your people aren't heard, they feel neither respected nor part of the team and your organization will struggle with communications and suffer all kinds of cooperation breakdowns as a result.

Make sure your people are being heard.

Appreciate Your People

Making sure your people know you appreciate them sounds remedial. But today more than ever, it's crucial.

Across the board, whenever your people do a good job, you want to make sure they know that you appreciate their good work and reward them for it along the way.

And by reward, I don't necessarily mean money.

Sure, everyone appreciates a little extra cash, and it's easy to say to yourself, "I'll just give that person a little bonus for a job well done." But as a leader, it's important for you to know your people and know what would be meaningful to them. Maybe money is good. But maybe public recognition is better, with you team members finding your public recognition of them more meaningful. Maybe they'd appreciate one-on-one time with you where you can express personally how you value them.

However you do it, be sure you say "thank you."

Never Embarrass Your People

Everybody makes mistakes. We all understand that, and we all repeat that saying until one of the people around us makes a mistake.

The very worst thing that you can do with your people is publicly scold them, talk them down, dress them down—whatever you want to call it when you publicly single someone out and make him or her look inferior in front of your other people. Whenever that happens, whenever you embarrass your people in front of others, the only thing they can do is defend themselves and feel angry because you've put them in a bad spot in front of everyone.

You need to have such discussions in private. And don't attack. Instead, ask what was going on. Gather information to understand why that person made that decision. Understand what exactly happened. Determine if the issue was a failure in that person's training, a lack of judgment, or simply an error—there are a thousand things that could go into it, but singling out and embarrassing people never works.

Respect your people. Things will go a lot better.

Focus on Building Strength

We all have both strengths and weaknesses.

There are different ideas and different mindsets about which one you should focus on. If you're like me, there are about 16 bazillion things you're terrible at. And of those, there are one or two things that, if you work on them, they'll help you develop and grow and become more.

In other words, you can work on eliminating weaknesses, or you can work on developing strengths.

So pick out those things you can work on. Connect with those who can help you and learn from them. One of the best things you can do for your organization is focus on your own personal growth.

Build your strengths.

Push Yourself

Let's assume that you're a talented individual, that you've learned how to do something and get better at it, and—whatever it is—people recognize you for it.

The problem with being talented is that a lot of times, people who are talented start to coast. They find the thing they do well, get comfortable with doing it, and settle for the money it pays.

"This," they tell themselves, "is as far as I want to go." And they start to kind of level off instead of pushing themselves.

I want to encourage you to keep pushing yourself.

You have talent (or you wouldn't be a leader). Figure out how to make your talent *shine*. One of the best ways to get better at what you do is to find someone you know who's both in your field and further along on the leader journey than you are. Develop a relationship with that individual and ask questions—"How did you get here?" "What mistakes have you made?" "What have you learned from them?" "What could have gone better?"

Use those lessons others have learned It allows us to push your talent and develop it even more.

What's Your Opinion?

What's your opinion of the people you work with?

As leaders, we start to form opinions about the people who work with us and work for us. We don't think about it, don't even realize we're doing it.

Sometimes that opinion is very high—"Man, she answered that exactly right!" or "Wow, he stepped right up, right place and took care of that issue!"

Sometimes that opinion goes very low—"He was really dragging on that task, wasn't he?" or "Gee, she really dropped the ball that time."

But here's what happens on the leadership level: whatever our opinion is of our people, that's how we start to lead them. The trouble with that is that it also becomes how they follow our leadership. Sure, it works out fine when they can tell their leader has a high opinion of them—they say to themselves, "I know the boss trusts me, so on this task, I'll really have to rise to the occasion."

However, when they know you lead them from a place of low opinion, their thoughts are more likely to go, "No matter how hard I try, it's never going to work, so what difference does it make?"

Your people will define themselves and set their attitudes about their work based on your opinion.

You don't need to treat everybody the same (in fact, you shouldn't—they're not all the same). But recognize that your opinion may actually be determining both your people's work ethics and how far they go in the organization.

Remember, everybody has bad days. Don't let their bad days define who they are for you—your opinions of them can change their outcomes.

Influence

What you do today influences what happens tomorrow.

This may seem obvious at first. But with that in mind ask yourself, "What are you doing today to get where you want to be tomorrow?"

What are the connections you're making? Who are you learning from? Whose influence is helping you grow? What have you learned to make you netter at what you're doing? Which people are shining the light for you? Which ones are blocking the sun and need to be pruned away?

It can be difficult to do that pruning. But one of the most important things for you to understand about your personal growth is that some of the people around you—sometimes even family—may become impediments to getting where we want to go, reaching our goals, and doing what it is we want to go in life.

Stay on your journey and do what you mist to make the most of what you've been given.

Developing Leaders Around You, Part 1: Characteristics Leaders Must Have

In his book, *Developing the Leaders Around You,* John Maxwell, talks about the characteristics that every leader must have. Whether you're leading or selecting others to lead, these characteristics, he says, are non-negotiable—you have to have them to be successful:

- Great people skills
- Positive attitude
- Influentialness
- Great character

If you look back over the different relationships you've had at work that maybe didn't go so well, I'll bet you any amount of money, marbles, or chalk—whatever you got in your pocket—that whenever there was a problem, it was because those other people were not developing an didn't these basic characteristics every leader needs to have.

People either have them or they don't, and even when they do have them, they may need to develop them. They may have strong character, but need to work on their people skills. That's okay. But when they don't have one of these characteristics to begin with, there are always going to be problems like the ones I asked you to recall a moment ago.

Whenever you're hiring people as leaders—whether a team leader, manager, VP or whatever—we want to be careful not to make excuses when we find they have much of what we want but lack one or more of these essential characteristics.

Whenever you find any of these basic characteristics that every leader lacking in a candidate, when it's simply not there in the individual, don't give them the benefit of the doubt in your hiring decision and find someone else.

Developing Leaders Around You, Part 2: The Quality of Gratitude

Whenever you're hiring, make sure that the people you're going to bring into your team have these four qualities:

- Resiliency
- Attitude of service
- Ability to follow through
- Gratitude

Of those four, I'm going to focus on gratitude.

Whether I'm reading a book, listening to an interview or perusing an article of some kind, what I'm finding more and more is that people who have this attitude of thankfulness, who stop and recognized the bigger picture and feel gratitude for what they have, those are the people you want in your organization.

People who have a thankful attitude generally have what most anybody would call a "great attitude."

As a leader, you want to make sure that the people you bring on to help lead have the qualities of resiliency, service, and follow-through—those are important for successful leaders in any organization. But it's so very critical that we stop from time to time and give thanks and that we recognize of the things that we have instead of dwelling on the things that we don't.

Hire people who have gratitude in life.

You Get What You Expect

You've heard this before.

You're going to find exactly what you're looking for in relationships with the people around you, whether that's social relationships, family relationships, or relationships with your coworkers.

If you're looking for problems, if you're looking for flaws, if you're looking for failures and screw ups and things people aren't doing, you're going to find them.

Conversely, if you're looking for successes, if you're looking for people who are making great strides in what they're doing, who are growing and developing and accomplishing the tasks that you send them out to do—even if there are mistakes, you'll find them as well.

As a leader, you're always going to find—and you're always going to get—what you're looking for in the people around you. Look for the negative, and that's what you'll find. Look for the positive, and you'll reinforce the positive wherever in your organization you look.

Being a Leader and Friend

Several years ago, a great leader who I knew was talking about the people on his leadership team. "A lot of the strife and problems, a lot of the egos, and whatever people struggle with on their teams, we don't have on my team because everybody on my team are all my friends."

That hit me like a sledgehammer.

Stunned by his revelation, I realized that it had never occurred to me to make my coworkers my friends. I didn't know it was at all *possible*.

Yes, it's not a hundred percent possible in every situation, but it might surprise you to know there's a lot you do have in common with your coworkers. In my own coaching, we identify that a lot of people have the same values as well as a lot of the same characteristics and qualities. They may show up a little differently because of environmental circumstances, but—man, oh man!—the people around us really could be some of our friends.

If we're ready.

At the end of the day, the people who serve alongside us, who we're going to spend at least a third of every work day with—perhaps we should get to know them and have a relationship with that's positive and supportive and helpful for both of us.

Allow people to be a friend to you. Start with being a friend to them first.

Leadership Focus: Your Strengths

What should you focus on in your leadership? Style? Skills? Weaknesses? Strengths?

There's all kinds advice and debates and arguments about what you should be looking at, but really it's a no brainer.

Focus on your weaknesses and, and really, really work on getting better or stronger, and chances are good chance that your weaknesses will remain your weaknesses—maybe less weak, sure, but your weakness still.

Focus on your strengths, the things you're really good at, talk to mentors and keep working that muscle or honing that edge, and that strength will make you stronger overall. You'll grow as a leader, and not only will you become stronger in the areas where you're already strong, but you'll become stronger in your weaker areas, too.

Focus on your strengths, and get better the things you're already good at. The rest will come along with it.

Dealing with People

Leadership is really pretty cool and could actually be even better if we didn't have to deal with all the people.

The problem with that thinking is that if you're not dealing with the people, you're not actually seeing anybody.

A lot of my coaching clients struggle with the people working with them. Those people are getting a paycheck, but they're not really producing as well as they could, which is really frustrating to the leaders.

So the leaders get frustrated—to the point where they sometimes make things worse.

When you get so frustrated that you can't see straight, *never do anything to make the situation worse.* As leader, it's your responsibility to know how to defuse a problem, even if you're so angry or so frustrated that you can bite nails in half.

That's why you're the leader.

Know how to apply the things you're learning when things get difficult. *Especially* when you're so angry or so frustrated that you can bite nails in half.

A Lesson on Purpose from *The West Wing*

As an aspiring leader, I always loved watching the TV series *The West Wing*.

There was drama. There was politics. There was always something to figure out. But the thing that was always most interesting to me was that, no matter what was going on in the story, whoever the staff was as the producers changed out the show's actors changed up the storyline or whatever else, there was never any misunderstanding among the characters about what they were there for.

They were there to serve the American people.

I always found that fascinating because whenever they were dealing with an issue, they dealt with it quickly and decisively. I remember several episodes where they talked about why they were there: To serve at the pleasure of the President in order to serve the American people.

Wow. Pretty straightforward.

If you were to ask the people that work with you in your organization, "What are we here for?" Could they say it that concisely?

We call that vision. It's the purpose of their work. It's the direction of the organization. And if your people don't know it, they'll be at the level that you want them to be.

Because they don't know where they're going.

Make sure your people know their purpose so they can do their jobs the best they can.

Who Have You Influenced Today?

Who have you influenced today?

John Maxwell says leadership is simply influencing others—nothing more, nothing less. So the question stands for you, as a leader: who have you influenced today, in a positive way? Who have you have made sure to pass along some nugget of truth to?

Leaders often get so caught up in dealing with the fires and the crises and the problems, the crunching the numbers and signing things that we forget that leadership is about inspiring and having an impact on the people we work with.

Who is it? Who is the person you made sure you've influenced today or to whom you've passed along something you've learned—from your victories or mistakes or anything you've just observed on your journey—so they can benefit?

If your answer is "I'm not sure," go pass along something you know to somebody. Today.

Training

One of things I hear all the time when I'm at a client site is, "I never was really trained on this."

It's one of the one of the easiest things for an organization to fall into. A manager has fifty different deadlines and is suddenly made responsible for some wide-eyed newbie just escorted into the office. That manager's response: "I don't have time for this." And the manager pulls the newbie aside, and says, "You've got this. It's not hard to understand. You'll be fine."

And leaves the new hire to figure it out alone. And you know what? That new hire won't be fine, and won't figure out the job without the help of someone who knows it.

It's very hard—and unfair—to hold people accountable to do a job they were never told or trained or shown how to actually do. If you want efficiency and good culture along with a phenomenal product, make sure you're training your people properly, right out of the gate. Or you're always going to be working on catch up and fixing things down the road.

Train your people right, at the beginning.

Define Communication

Whatever it is you're communicating about, make sure you define it.

When you're communicating, especially at the workplace, it's your responsibility to make sure that that any and all terms are clearly defined. Ask yourself:

"What are we talking about?"

"What is the thing that we're discussing?"

"What's the subject matter?"

"Are we all in agreement on this?"

You need to ensure that everybody's on that same page about whatever decision is being communicated. The best way to do that? Say it over and over and over again, twenty times if you have to—people won't hear it the first several times, just because of the all the distractions their own day and their own lives are throwing at them.

You're the leader. You're responsible for making sure whatever is being communicated is also understood.

Make sure you define the terms within your discussions.

Focus on Strengths

Many moons ago, in a galaxy far, far away, I was told by people who both meant well and actually kind of knew what they were doing that I need make that I understood what my strengths and my weaknesses are, and focus on my weaknesses, because anything I'm not good at, I need to get better at. And that made sense to me.

Even though it's untrue.

We all have things that we're very, very...not so good at.

But we also have things we're extraordinary at. Something we do at a higher level than anyone around us. Better than any 10,000 other people.

Do you think it makes sense to focus on one of your weaknesses?

Sure, work on them from time to time. But focus on those things you're fantastic at so you get even better at them—the better you can get at them, the more you can offer and the more you can help, the more you can make a difference in other people's lives.

Know your strengths and weaknesses. But focus on your strengths.

Give Feedback

Give your team your feedback.

Not just any feedback, given any way. You need to set an example for giving feedback—especially positive feedback. Be a good finder. Whenever your people are doing something well, tell them.

Make sure they know that you see it and that you appreciate it.

Multiplicity of Leadership

As I've already discussed, leadership is influence. Nothing more, nothing less. What you need to understand, though, is how far that influence can spread.

Whenever you influence somebody—have an effect on somebody, particularly when it's in a positive way—that effect is more far-reaching than just the one person you influenced. It stretches out from that one person in an enormous web of influence, multiplying the number of lives your influence touches as well.

How many? I've read different numbers, but here's the striking one: Even an introvert who basically secludes himself and limits severely the number of people he interacts with will still over a lifetime go on to influence 10,000 other people.

That's the introvert. If you're out and about, going to meetings, visiting client sites, maybe even occasionally speaking at industry events, what multiplicity applies to your influence? How many people's lives do you think you're touching, without even realizing it?

The more you grow, the more you learn, the deeper you become, and the greater your strengths become. And the multiplicity kicks in, the more you positively influence everybody else.

Go out in the world and use your influence to change lives.

Learn from the Leaders Around You

As a leader, it's your responsibility to make sure that you're learning from people who are smarter than you, are more developed than you are, or just farther along in their journey and even just a little more experienced than you are.

Face-to-face is the best way to do this, but we have so many other opportunities, whether it's through books, podcasts, webinars, or video series. Whatever the best way to get this information to you, make time to be learning from other people.

Even if you learn from them that whatever it is they did or experienced is something you don't want to go through.

The more you connect with other leaders, the more you learn what they've dealt with and the fights they've had and the struggles they've overcome—all the things that they've gone through, the more you'll see it's all the same stuff you're dealing with.

We're all in this together. The more we connect, the more we learn, the stronger and more confident of a leader we become.

Learn from the leaders around you.

What Are You Prepared to Do?

In the 1987 movie *The Untouchables*, Sean Connery's character Jimmy Malone begins and ends his relationship with his protégé, Untouchables leader Elliot Ness (Kevin Costner), with one question:

"What are you prepared to do?"

It's an important question for a leader.

What are you prepared to do? For your team, for your project, for the task that need to get done? Are you ready to work all night? To search out needed information? To learn a new skill you need to complete a project? To admit you don't know what you're doing and need to track down a resource who knows what to do? To take your entire organization to the next level?

What are you prepared to do? What a phenomenal question.

What's your answer?

Pull the Trigger

As a leader, there are times when you have to make "The Decision."

You have to decide for your organization whether to go left or right, or all in or pull back, to stay where you are or push on through.

Should you assemble all the facts and make pros and cons list? Or just go with your gut.

Yes.

Not the answer you want to hear, but yes. As a leader, you need to always be gathering information and weighing options so you can make the right decision at the right time. Also as a leader, you have to develop your intuition and know that sometimes, when all the facts point one way but the little voice in the back of your mind screams for you to go the other, you have to listen to that little voice.

The one thing you can't do is wait. Whether it's analysis paralysis demanding more data or plain fear of making the wrong call, there are decisions only you can make.

You have to make the call to go one way or the other. Nobody else can make these decisions, nor should they. That's why you're in charge. That's why you're the leader.

Pull the trigger.

Get the Job Done

As the leader, It's you job to see that the job gets done.

It doesn't matter how much you have to do. It doesn't matter how late you have to stay. It doesn't matter how much you have to accomplish to finish what needs to be finished.

All that matters is that the job gets done. And you have to get the job done, no matter what.

You're responsible.

Get it done.

Being a Leader

Leader is more than a title.

As John Maxwell has pointed out, there are people who lead regardless of their title, and people in positions of leadership who do not lead.

A label doesn't make for a leader. If you're influencing the people around you, if your actions and words have an impact and inspire those around you to do better, you're leading. And if you're not having that impact and providing that inspiration, regardless of your title, you're no leader.

Don't worry about your title. Set making a difference as your goal and live your life and do your work in a way that inspires those around you.

Lead.

Understand Your Leadership Strengths

Leadership is kind of a catch-all word. Often when we use it, it means whatever the speaker and listener think it to mean in phrases such as "We must be strong leaders" or "We need to take inventory of out gifts as leaders"—with no real context to define it so we all know what we're talking about.

Let's break it down a little bit.

Different leaders possess different leadership gifts. There are those who are great organizers—they can organize things, people, events, situations. There are some who are phenomenal at supporting and encouraging people, and there are still others who are great with strategy, at thinking through all the different aspects that go into that sort of planning.

What are your leadership strengths? Take an inventory, not just of your leadership strengths, but of those of the people around you, and look for how you can all come together to make your team even stronger.

Figure out your strengths as a leader. Understand how the make you unique in handling the things you do.

Communication Details

If you're a leader like me, you find you I have trouble with details.

I'm reminded regularly of my inability to slow down, to stop and read the fine print or catch a specific point in a conversation. It's come back to bite me in the backside. More than once.

Even if you're a great communicator, if it's one of your strengths as a leader, it's easy to browse the details—especially when communicating with your own people. It's simple and straightforward, and you assume they "got" what you said and you move on to the next thing.

But you're not always as good as you think you are. You skim over this part of your explanation, miss a few numbered steps in another—in your mind, it's pretty simple, and you've gone over parts of it with them before...

When you find yourself starting to brush by the details, stop. Take a breath. And then make sure you have communicated all the details.

All of them.

It's hard for me to do that, and it may be hard for you. But it's critical that your people hear everything you want them to understand.

Make sure you communicate the details.

Strengths and Weaknesses

We always have to be adjusting what we're doing to the circumstances around us.

But there's a problem.

Whenever circumstances begin to control the outcome of the vision for your organization, how do you adjust? When do we pull the trigger and make the adjustment? When do we adjust?

The way to reach that answer comes back to knowing who you are through the Values Conversation, and understanding the leadership gifts you have but also recognizing the vision of your organization.

As a leader, you must always be adjusting. You're constantly moving the things that are in the way so your organization can grow and become more, deciding when to move them, how to move them, and in what direction to move them.

Don't let circumstances control the vision.

Abundance of Resources

You're a leader, so you know the pain of finding resources to solve a problem.

"Where can we go?" "What does the solution look like?" "How many people can we talk to?" "What does that mean?" "Do we have the resources?" and on and on and on. It's frustrating like hitting your head against the wall.

Here's the truth, though: The resources are going to be there.

One way or the other, in large part based on your attitude, the resources are going to be there. If you believe there aren't enough resources, or that you just don't know enough people or that just not enough people care, guess what? The resources won't be there.

But if you keep pushing, if you keep asking and searching, you will find the answer. The resource you need will manifest and you will find that person you need to talk to or that extra pair of hands.

The answer is always there. You either find it or don't based on the attitude and the energy and effort you put into solving the problem you're facing.

Assume the resource you need is there, and find it.

A Leader's Role

Why do people in leadership roles become jealous or intimidated or scared by somebody else's success?

You would think a leader would simply say, "So they're doing well and they things going in the right direction. Good for them."

But instead, they become upset by that. Again, why?

Do a check-up on your own attitude toward the success of your peers and the people around you—especially if you're responsible for them. If they're growing or developing, or they're having success at their job, or if they're just getting things going the way that you want them to go, don't ask yourself, "Why not me?" Don't ask yourself "Why am I not the one getting all the success?"

Instead, do what a leader does: Being happy for their success.

Take Responsibility

I'm pretty sure at some point, you've screwed up.

Royally.

You dropped the ball, screwed up, crashed and burned—you did the completely wrong thing at precisely the wrong time in the exactly wrong way.

And you were told, never to do that ever again.

What do you do now?

When you're a leader, when you make mistakes, the buck stops with you. That's what leadership is: taking responsibility.

Weak leaders are people who are in over their head and always play the victim. As soon as a situation start to go off course, they start looking for somebody to blame. Or maybe some circumstances to point to that may have affected the outcome.

All those things may have actually happened. But it's a leader's responsibility to overcome those obstacles and make sure, whatever the effort it, that it continues to advance and the organization can accomplish its goals.

We're all human, and we're all going make mistakes. The question for you as a leader is:

How do I respond when I made the mistake?

Fostering the Right Kind of the Team

John Maxwell has a story about developing a cough while traveling to a speaking event in South Africa. He tells how, on his way into the event—where he'd be speaking for hours—the cough was particularly bothering him. One of his team members reached in his pocket and produced a cough drop for him, and Maxwell expressed his surprise at the fact that it was not only the exact brand he would have bought for himself, but that his team member happened to have cough drops on him at all.

The team member shrugged. "All of us are carrying cough drops."

What a phenomenal team, right?

What are you doing to foster that consideration in your team? That would lead them to be ready to do what needs to be done, whether completing a report at the last minute or having your brand of cough drops on hand?

Are you doing what you need to, as a leader, to get that that level?

Don't Have All the Answers

I hear a lot from leaders how they get frustrated by their team always coming to them asking questions and looking for answers.

I hate to tell them, but when that's happening, there's a pretty good chance that it's because their team's been trained to do that.

If you give people the answers, they'll keep coming back to you for answers people.

You see, it's a mistake to solve their problems for them—then they don't learn to solve problems themselves. It's a fine line when you're a leader to protect the organization from people's mistakes and letting your people sometimes fail and make the mistakes they need to in order to learn and become more effective in their jobs. But as a leader, it's your responsibility to find that fine line.

Let your people struggle, learn, and grow from the mistakes and the opportunities that land in front of them.

Proper Timing

I overheard a gentleman at a diner telling another gentlemen, his thoughts about God and the Bible and so on and so forth.

Now, I was a minister for 30 years and I know a couple of things about theology and the Bible. And as I listened to him, I wasn't agreeing with the great philosophical, theological truth he was expounding. It was mostly BS, but as much as I thought about stepping in and showing him the scripture that he was missing, I didn't do any of that. I just sat there, drinking my coffee, looking at my phone, waiting for the client I was there to meet.

Because it wasn't the right time for me to have that theological conversation with that gentlemen.

Timing is essential in communication. When you need to communicate information to your people, it's your responsibility as leader to not only say the right thing, but to say it at the right time.

Always say what needs to be said. But always say it at the proper time.

Provide Direction

What provides needed direction to the people you work with? The employee handbook? The company policy manual? Industry regulations?

The one answer most people, even leaders, won't come up with is the organization vision.

The vision is set by leadership it should overshadow every other company reference and source of direction—even those regulations, as they should have informed the vision in the first place.

Without the vision, your team can't understand what they're expected to ultimately accomplish. Everything they do, whether for customers or co-workers, ties back to the vision.

What's your vision?

Learning Never Stops

I grew up in a little town in Southern Missouri. When I was a senior in high school, I remember how my friends and I couldn't wait to be done with school. We talked all the time about how, once we graduated, we would never, ever, ever, never, ever, ever, *ever* go back to school again. Well, maybe college, but after that we would be done with school.

When are we really done with school?

Never

Wherever you are in your professional career, if you're not learning, if you're not still "going to school in some fashion, you're just hampering your professional understanding and growth.

You must be learning constantly. Whether in-person, through books, podcasts, webinars, or video series, whatever you find is the best way for you to get information to you, make time to learn from other people.

As a leader you're always going to be learning, always going to be growing, always going to be "going to school."

Embrace it.

Stuck Behind an Inferior Leader

What do you do if you're stuck behind an inferior leader?

Most of the time, people in that position fall into some kind of victimized "Woe is me! I can't believe how terrible this is!" attitude.

Which accomplishes nothing.

So what do you do? First thing, recognize the one thing you have complete control over is your attitude. Check it, set it, and resolve yourself to one simple thing: *You will control that which you can control.* There are a lot of things you can do and whatever those things are, focus on them. Create something positive out of the negative situation and create what you must, one step at a time, without being a victim.

Let the rest go.

Problem People

There's one key thing that you can do when dealing with problem people:

Try to get to know them.

You'll be amazed how, once you get to know somebody who irritates or hacks you off—whether an employee or associate or coworker—and understand where they're coming from, that suddenly they smarten up and they're not so dumb or grating as they once were.

You have to try.

And if you're a leader, it's part of your job to know your people, employees and peers, and build relationships with them.

Understand what the people around you are thinking, what their various perspectives are and why.

Bottlenecks

It's easy for a leader to get in the way of progress.

The easiest way to keep things moving when the stack of tasks gets too high is to delegate. But we're often afraid to and we make excuses not to.

Which hurts the people on our team.

When you don't delegate, they don't get to do their jobs. Worse yet, they don't get to stretch beyond their jobs by helping. They don't get to learn new things and they don't get the opportunity to deliver and accomplish more than they thought they could.

If you don't know when to delegate, assess your people. And if you find you have people who, on any give task you do, can do that task at 80% capacity or more, give it to them.

You read that right. If they can accomplish a task at least 80% of what you can do, hand that responsibility off and seek out something else you can handle—as the leader the more you offload, the more time you free up to it to do what you really should be doing.

The things that others can't do.

Don't be the bottleneck. Delegate out what you can and trust your people.

Let them learn, grow, and develop

Are You a Manager or a Leader?

Leader and *manager* somehow get used interchangeably in business settings.

But they're not the same thing.

Another word for *manager* is *maintainer*. Often, managers don't lead—they maintain—and there's nothing wrong with that.

As long as expectations are understood.

A manager maintains a team or system or segment of an organization. A manager makes sure things run smoothly, and that all the moving parts keep moving the way they're supposed to.

An important job, for sure. But it's not *leadership*.

A leader increases the energy. A leader excites people and lifts them up. A leader helps creativity flow, opens the door for more ideas, thoughts, programs, innovations, or whatever else. A leader pushes and drives things forward.

Managers need leaders—someone needs to create the vision and provide the environment for innovation. Leaders absolutely need managers—someone needs to make sure the fine print is read and that the *i*'s are dotted and the *t*'s are crossed.

Which are you?

Which is your team looking for?

Making the Key Decision at the Key Time

In the movie *The Post*, Meryl Streep plays Katharine Graham, publisher of the *Washington Post* and depicts her paper's effort and her decisions around publishing the infamous Pentagon Papers, classified documents detailing the involvement of the U.S. government in the Vietnam War.

All politics aside, it was a big moment in the history of the nation, a big moment in the history of that newspaper, and a big moment in Katharine Graham's leadership.

It's really the story of how she grows into her leadership. She struggles to understand her place until she has to make the decision to publish the documents or not. Once she makes that decision, she's set, she's focused, and she steps into the leadership role.

Waiting until a decision finds you is too late. You need to be ready when that decision comes up. You need to be preparing and growing as a leader because, sooner or later, a decision will come that you—and only you, as the leader—have to make.

Prepare now for when that decision comes up.

Solving Problems

As a leader, part of your job is to teach your people how to solve problems.

You solve problems all the time, whether it's fixing a communications breakdown in your organization, running down an equipment issue with a supplier, meeting a sudden customer request, settling a dispute between two members of your team, or just making sure everything's running smoothly day to day.

But is the problem you're solving really the problem?

Often, the problem that presents itself is just a symptom of a much bigger issue. Solving it perhaps puts an end to the immediate situation, but doesn't do anything to address the larger, underlying issue. Think of it as putting out a fire but leaving smoldering embers laying everywhere.

The fire's going to flare back up.

When a problem crops up, instead you jumping in to solve it, take a look at it, and put your team on it to identify and address the bigger issue underlying it. It's your responsibility to discern who should be handling which problems.

Step back sometimes, and let your people handle it.

Lead Through a Turnaround

Nina DiSesa of the McCann Erickson ad agency identified four consistent factors in any turnaround situation:

- Morale is going to be low.
- Fear is going to be high
- Good people are halfway out the door
- Slackers are in hiding

Of course, there are always a lot more things going on as well. But those four are true in any situation, in any company, in any team, in any department. And it's your responsibility as leader to be able to recognize these factors and head them off.

I'll warn you: especially if you're brought into the situation from the outside, these factors are always present, and they will jump out to bite you on the behind at some point.

So you need to be prepared.

Take an honest look at the problems. Make decisions. Turn the team around, and take it where it needs to go.

Be a leader.

More Success, More Problems

The more successful we can become in business, the more problems we encounter.

After the attack on September 11, 2001, former General Electric CEO Jeff Immelt, said, "My second day as chairman, a plane that I lease, flying with engines that I built, crashed into a building that I insure, and it was covered all with a network that I own."

That was a bad day. A bad situation. Bad circumstances. But as a leader, your responsibility is to be prepared on an emotional and mental and physical level to deal with those problems, whenever they arise. Sometimes we can see problems as they're coming. Sometimes we don't see it coming at all.

But it's still your responsibility to respond, to gather your people, go where you need to go and do what you.

It's your job to solve problems in a way that takes care of everybody and offers them all the support they need. Whether you saw the problem coming or not.

Be prepared.

The Weakest Link on Your Team

You like your people. You've connected with many of them, and have some kind of relationship with all of them.

So, as a leader, how do you deal with your team's weakest link?

You have to. Your team nearly all know who this person is, and you're undermining your credibility with all of them every day you put off dealing with that one person. And you have a responsibility to your organization to resolve it as well.

Be the leader they all need you to be.

Make the decision.

Emotions and Decisions

I don't know about you, but I've ended up in trouble every time I've made a decision based on emotion—when I was upset or angry or frustrated—I eventually find out that the decision I made really wasn't the smartest thing

We all know this.

But what we don't think about is that decisions made when we're emotional in the other direction—when we're ecstatic or thrilled or overjoyed—we can make decisions we later regret as well.

When your emotions are out at the extremes—high or low—you don't do your "due diligence" on a decision, skipping research or analysis or even questions and just go with the feeling.

Which can work out just as badly.

When you're a leader, it's your responsibility to put emotion aside and evaluate your options properly before making a decision.

Keep your feelings in check, and make sure you're making decisions after properly weighing the options.

Make Do With What You Have

Everybody wishes they had more resources.

"If we just purchased that new piece of equipment..."

"If we just move to a bigger building..."

"If we could just hire more people..."

"If we just find stronger experts..."

"If we could just implement that new technology..."

"If we just had this...we'd be able to do that—whatever this and that are.

There may actually be some truth in those formulations. But the hard reality is that no matter where we are, no matter what we accomplished, no matter how far we go, there are always more resources we could put toward accomplishing more.

As the leader, that's not what you're there to do.

Your responsibility is to get the job done with what you have. You don't have time to sit and daydream about what you could have or what you could do "if we just"—it's no excuse for not accomplishing what you need to.

Keep focused and keep moving forward with the resources you already have.

Step Up

You've seen when things go well for a sports team—when they take a division or conference title or win a championship—they're given accolades, and people talk about how the team came together and how they excelled.

But have you noticed when something goes wrong—when there are player injuries, when it's error after error on the field and there were losses at key points on the season—the coaches, the good coaches, step forward and take responsibility. "I didn't do a good job," they say. "I didn't have my coaching staff where they needed to be." or "I didn't have the team prepared like I should have."

Or, "It's all my fault."

Great leaders step back and let their people take the credit and enjoy the honors because great leaders know that their people are the one who got everything done.

And when things go wrong, great leaders step up and take the blame.

When you're the leader it's your responsibility to make sure things go right. It's your responsibility to let them know when they do things right and to thank them for it.

It's also your responsibility to protect them. So when things don't go right, you have to take the hit.

Always understand: The buck stops with you

Watch Your Mouth

The worst thing that you can do as a leader is to be gossiping about somebody who's gone.

First, you don't always know the truth, so what you're saying is basically uninformed. Second, whatever you say often going to get back to that person. Third, your people see that you talk about others when they're not around and start to wonder what they say about them behind their backs.

That will undermine and cut their trust in you more quickly than anything else.

What if the person who left is an idiot? Maybe, but that person's gone now, so who cares? And, like almost everything in life, you don't know all the details. We've all been "idiots" at some point in our lives, so give that person who's gone the benefit of the doubt. Don't worry about him or her anymore and instead focus on building up the people around you.

Protect the integrity of your team.

Self-Awareness

Great leaders are not only aware of what they're doing and what's going on. They're also aware of their surroundings and even more importantly, they're aware of their people and what's happening in their lives.

I was impressed when I heard St. Louis Cardinals coach Mike Matheny discuss in an interview how, as the season wore on, they would work to rearrange travel schedules for their players so they could stay home in St. Louis for family events such as school plays or student band concerts. The player would simply take a different flight and catch up with the team and be there for the away game.

Are you that aware of your people's lives? And considerate enough of their needs to massage their schedules that way to support them in their personal lives?

Let them know that you appreciate them and let them know how important they are to the team.

Be aware not just of your surroundings, but of your people, too.

Getting Along with Your Team

"No one is going to go along with you until they *can* get along with you."

Did your mother ever tell you that? Your grandfather, or a teacher maybe?

Here's the add-on to that: No one is going to follow you until they know who you are and how important they are to you.

As the leader, you have to be able to walk the line and balance leading your people, setting the vision, giving directives, and being respectful of who they are and what they need. Do you know the people on your team and their lives? Do you know their personalities? What makes them tick and what motivates them?

Some of them want more money. Some want recognition. Some just want a little extra time off. Some want something I'm not even thinking of because they're not my team.

They're yours.

What makes them tick? What makes them get even more excited about what you're doing together as a team?

Your team needs you to find out.

They need you to find out so they can get along with you better—and so that you can get along with them. Be purposeful in creating the environment for that mutual discovery so you can become more cohesive as a group, as an organization and as a company.

Learn about your team.

Know the Winds

> "The pessimist is the one who's always complaining and criticizing the wind. The optimist is the one who's always positively convinced that the wind is going to change. The leader is the one who adjusts the sails to what the wind is doing."

That's how John Maxwell sums a great leader.

You can dig in your heels and talk about what used to be and insist it's what you know and it's the way it has to be.

Do that, and you're already obsolete.

You can also be so forward-thinking that you miss what's going on today, where you stand and what your present circumstances are.

Lean that far forward, and you'll fall on your face.

Great leaders know where they're coming from, but aren't limited by it. They keep an eye toward their destination, even if it's over the horizon, but always know where they are so they can set a course and adjust the sails to get them where they're going.

Are you adjusting your sails?

Walk Them Through It

For any leader, delegation is a big deal.

"Do I hand this off?" "Do I delegate this assignment?" "Are they ready to take on this task?" "Is the team prepared for this kind of work?" "Is this person ready?"

There's a very simple method to apply when delegating, to help whoever you're delegating to become ready for the new responsibility. It's just four steps:

Step One: I do it.

Step Two: I do it, you watch.

Step Three: You do it, I watch.

Step Four: You do it.

Using this method, you walk your people through whatever task you want them to take on—in stages. Doing it this way gives you both a chance to observe and be observed so that you're both thinking and asking questions. I also allows you to become the "training wheels" for your people as you encourage them learn new things, improve their skills and grow.

Delegate. First walk them through it, then hand them responsibility for it.

About the Author

Founder of THE VALUES CONVERSATION, Jeff Arthur is a highly accomplished and experienced executive coach. He has worked with Fortune 500 companies/CEOs as well as small/medium business owners and entrepreneurs.

From the inception of The Values Conversation, Jeff has asserted that personal coaching is a central component of the program and he continues to coach individuals as part of his daily responsibilities.

Made in the USA
Columbia, SC
18 March 2022